A POET OF
NO FIXED
AGENDA

A POET OF NO FIXED AGENDA

Jon Sutcliffe

authorHOUSE®

AuthorHouse™ UK Ltd.
1663 Liberty Drive
Bloomington, IN 47403 USA
www.authorhouse.co.uk
Phone: 0800.197.4150

Published by AuthorHouse 07/12/2013

ISBN: 978-1-4817-7002-6 (sc)
ISBN: 978-1-4918-0004-1 (e)

Contents

MEMORIES AND MISERIES

Laura-lye Laura-Leigh

She, in a fit of wisdom—imprinted upon me
The illusion of tomorrow
                    The Day and the Next
And the precious nature of the time
                    In between.

And I suddenly realized the thief I had been

And the now damaged quality—All the
                    Time I stole
                    Quantified itself in an aching instance

With its disappearance.

I, In a gap of new found poverty—stricken
In a timeless deficit
                    The past and the rest
Made meaningless with memory now transparent
                    Like Air.

Climbing from the gap that's made for those

With nothing but time to spend—All the
                    Time I stole
                    Infinitely itself an aching distance

Now Nigh
          Laura-lye
          I, too long astray
                    Laura-Leigh.

Then, To begin an Ageless Epiphany—Potential to live a mere
forever
                    The Leash or Tether's
Just torn leather reigns in flames and ashes
                    Like Halo's

In a perpetual Orgasm of possibility, Scope
And argued reality—All the
                    Time I stole
In love with itself after the voids clearance

Leaving trace and faintness as reward

Now, In reach at a stretch—before the image of illusion settles
to shape tomorrow
                    A Day and A Next
A precious nature to replace the damage's
                    The Decay
It's spinning reels of improper misfortune—A tax of its own
gamble—All the
                    Time I stole
                    Now fruitless itself—Void—A lost endurance

Pay no price to play—or too high

Now Nigh
           Laura-Lye
           No longer Astray
                    Laura-Leigh

As, the birds begin to Herald—Tomorrow and the
Lurid tides of dawn
                    Fresh scent and breath
Forward pathways emerge on the ground
                    Like canvas

The end where New worlds collide along a Journey for returns
purpose—All the
                    Time I stole
            Providing for me in life's travel—a pittance

New gambles to be made—Potentially lost or Won

And upon Return at Journeys End—Through shambled messes
or woes
                    Unscathed and Saved
As maps meander Round Robins, full circle
                    And Entwine

The waste and time will pass with time to waste—leaving no
warranty—All The
                    Time I stole
            Bidding for itself to rest—A good Riddance

Now time to endure
            A purpose or two
                    Now Nigh
                            Laura-Lye
                            Lead me never astray
                                    Laura-Leigh

Before, setting and travelling into the night—Rafael—as my
Watchman
                    Lanterns and starlight
We strode as if still lover's to
The shore

The Ebbing of the gentle waves crashing with delicate
Echoes—All the
                    Time I stole
            Into the sea washed clean—from existence

In its Memory and place—The Joy of the embrace

To the summit of the earth—The depths of the ocean

Where time and solitude shape and
Color into twinned lupines

Into a cave by the light of harvest moons—we shall witness
each other, A last time—All the
                    Time I stole

Struck a final chord—An Epiphany—Remembrance

It resonates, there
            Now in Harmony
To sing in nights forgotten
                    Laura-Lye
                    To settle the days
                            Laura-Leigh

Who Was She?

The one who never arrived
        The image and
            Visage
Who has torn me to pieces

Just to never arrive
        Existence was cheated

A Poets Anguish

Self slanderous Vernacular
        I'm still worried for my sanity

I am well—but in feeling, I am
        Ill—Tomorrow darker still
And Nightmares—of drowning
          Ruined Ribcages
      Missing Jaws
          And a loose eyeball
The bank against the crashing
        Sea—where my broken skull
        Will bloody the muddy
          Waters
Again
      I slipped
          Into Anguish

A collection of Ceremonies

The Harmless Charms, In Palms—Of a new aged
Heralds stern alarms
                    In a voice of calm
And measured Merit

Sat before his lord—In a
                    Meditative silence

As a busying world
                    Waned
Far from the busier sounds
                    In his mind
A finalizing Statement

Obscure observation creates
Through obscurity whilst
Accuracy destroys the limit
Of the observed
An element itself is of an element
Itself

            Elemental Until

                    Reaction

                        And Chaos

Both of which
Are elements
            Themselves

A Nature by Virtue

I foresaw my Judgment in the eternities
                        After my Death
The Rivers, Fountains
                        And Fires
The Circles—The Hoards and Masses
                        Of the Damned
        I saw Myself Suspended

As the Fortune Tellers were forever
                Travelling Backwards

        Gates Delving into Darkness

        The Heat Dense

A Poet's Bug

Damn—I'm inspired again with a slant
                    An Alternative Story
            Millions and Trillions of
                    Accounts of Events

The Imagery Rages
            Rattles Cages

The Descript sense to
        Convey and Play

                The Idea of Toys
                To Toy with Idea's

My Mind Never growing numb
            Of tiny Innovations
                    Spawning Creations

This seemingly never ceasing

                Tiring

        Awfully Inspiring

                Bug.

An Explanation

What are any of these
            Mythologies?
To a Poet
            Playing with
With Myths

A Mythological Poet
Perhaps?
            Shakespeare
or Virgil
Or Dante—His Inferno

Maybe it's Heaven
            In stark Contrast
                        Elsewhere
            In Time

On more mythological
Pages
By Other
            Mythological
Poets

            Playing with
                        Myths

An Insanity Incarnate

Rogue thought. Contagion Agent
      This Introduction Speech
            The Death in Ten Words
The First Humor,
         Then in Twos and Threes
And a Riddle;
      After you've died—
           Where have you been?
And Three doors
      Two of which—Walk you out the
           Door—You have to choose
This Tiny Maze

Panic, sets the spark,
         Compulsions and Obsessions
Electrons and Neurons
      Swirling—The idea's, Concepts its
           Constructions—building
Devastations
      A Shifting compound
         Now—Ever Evolving
           —Mutating
The atomic Implosions
         —Radioactivity
      Surrounding reality
         Absorbing into the
           Riddle Medley

Through a Calandria—In a Nuclear
Reaction
To appear through Blackholes
In the universes of minds
Appearing Elsewhere in Dreams
Or inspiration

I growing to be just a genius clown
Hung up in noose against the moon
The night is my only comfort
As my life in all its intricacies
Mind, Soul, Spirit
Scatter from me—In Ashes, Snow
Moths, Butterflies—Swords and shields
Till Limp and Lowered

Another Account

You can't blame a fool
    For falling
       In Love
Then growing ever the fool
Within
There
No Lover to held or
    Sung for
   Or Joy shared
    Spent
A fool—

When shall I meet her?
    I cried

She—Though in all daring
   Conceived
    Or placed
  For Players
   In Terms
  So Vain

Shall always exist
   Somewhere
For a Fool Such
As
 I

Bonfires for Vanities

(An Ironic Idyll)

Cast beneath——Engulfed
        Swallowed Below
As coal or salt
Into Arena's carved of Bone And
                          Stone
A Basin
        Sank within the Soil
Gallows'——Made of Rotted limb's
        Jutting into Mangled
                Manacles
My Sin of Suicide
        Torn in
Incoherent screams
Passing through my throat
        As Fire,

With each attempt to
        Stifle
——A thousand Stab wounds
        Strangle
    The strength
        To stop
    The Sentence

As reels of pages flood the Arena
    As Demon's Succubus
             And Imps
    To Fan the flames

Death's an Aphrodisiac

She drew me close to her
　　　　As fear wept—along with the brazen
　　　　　　Beating of her bereft heart

Breath after Breath after shallow breath
　　　　And beating, pounding breast

Salty tear's mixed within racing tongues
　　　　　　Outrunning Death's
　　　　　　　　Lingering Presence

　　　　Fresh in Mind

I caught a glimpse of her
　　　　As Lust swept—Awash in the uproar
　　　　　　Of a Lover's aching Void
　　　　　　　　To Fill

Breath after Breath after shallow breath
　　　　And beating, Pounding Breast

Mourning Moan's and the rampant longing
　　　　To Pace and Set
　　　　　　The distance between
　　　　　　　　Death's lingering
　　　　　　　　　　Presence

　　　　Fresh in Mind

17

Idea's like fleas/ No rhymes

Flying Fucks flew through my windows—
Crashed and burned—
And from the cinders rose this gentle notion pretending to be emotion that scorched the walls with words—
These words grew too much for the mindless assailant as he searched the remnants of his shattered mind for clues to what he might think he should do—
And as he lost himself further through the looking glass—
His spirit sprinted through the tragedy to the other side of morning—
Left bereft and free of hope he began to drown beneath the bare light bulb that swayed in the breeze

I tried to find her
She was gone

Broken Jaws and my skull felt
Like it had fallen apart

Splintered teeth and bone
Crunched in time
With my batting eyelids

The gathering had known
Buzzing they did depart

I looked around to take her
Beckoning
The bedroom bids

She was gone left
Taking with her
My broken heart

I sat in growing darkness
Numbed against
The glow—dim lit

Left in whispers
To cars—as I
Strummed my cards

A tapping of the glass
Shadows of strangers
And trumpets

She was gone
And the end now starts

I wander out in trust
Instincts dead
Empty, cold, Unhidden

No last warmth
The last ceremony to
Save this Soul
A Lover to wash
And purge
This sin

Incubus

I remember the night—In a dream
        Another Disguise
    Of Shadow's and
          Voodoo Masks

I Hung above her—As a creature
        Of Damned Design
    Thirsting Deep—for Flesh
In a slight Fear
    Of my own Haunted
Lust

In The Rafter's, This Capsule
        The Perimeters Dreaming
          Off into a Haze
    She Slept
      In A Red Gown
    Upon Lilac Sheets

I Held myself high above

    Tortured and Taunted

    By Her Beauty

    Forever Waiting

      The Dream to turn
        To Dust

Jack and Jill

The harmonious Harmony
Of a harmless harmonica
Could you imagine?
A night darker than tonight
Would you please?
Sit with me

Until your sun bursts through
Nurse me
Not curse me

And will I finally see
The warmth

The sanctimonious sacrosanct
Of a sanities sanctity
Shed a skin
Too tight—heathen flight
Would you please?
Sit with me

Until it grows again anew
Nurse me
Not curse me

With new skin finally feel
The Warmth

Love in Ransom Notes

Seven Months—I tore the Letter left
        From its darkened grave

            In its disused state—To reflect
                Upon the neglect

            The last inspection—timed, aligned
                    With my growing self destruction
                        Its function;
            Taxing my Overtures—Misery
                In Contemplation
            The Love it had offered
                Still held to
                    Ransom

The addressed perfectly and
                Equally torn envelope—Now
                    A mere sleeve let
                        A tomb
            And breaking the senses built
                To fight despair

            Measuring its overwhelming Price
                Paid—with its long term
                    Ransom In
                        Meaninglessness

            Drew up another Note—
                    For a Letter

Michael's last Proverb

I am Abel
> With annoying talents

To seem
> The image of a man

> More loved by God

Gentle in his embrace

Now saint of
> Self sacrifice

Moon Cycles

Growth, Destruction
And spin and cycle
I suppose it's like the dark
Side of the moon
Forever made Cold and forced
      Into harboring jealous secrets
Of Love, fancy and lust
      For its counterpart of famed
            Beauty

The dark side of the moon—seeming tamed
      Within the stillness
            And silence
Forced against the beautiful
      Sun forever
To contemplate the infinities
      Of the cosmos

Musing upon its intricacies
      As it turns and turns
            Again
Until a master of designs
      Conception
            Itself
Like a moth
      Trapped inside
            A Watch
Playing with its
      Own shadow

Night and its tricks

In the dark oblivion—Alone with no other
        Mind and its sense
                To assuage and assure
        Ease and cure
                Bring a light to shine
Within the cavern
        Of night

A misplaced thought—And its tricks
        Begin to tingle as they tangle
                Writhe and wrangle
        Mismanage and Mangle

One last happy Birthday

The final doused flames
Of a year long heart
    Burning with
    Pride against
    A dying light

Of romantic nights
And beauty's flights
    Deserved rests
    Again in
    Nests of fires
    And kites

The drowned mane
In a winters rain
    The slipping
    Trip—now and
    Again doused
    And drowned
        Again

Pest Controllers and the River Styx

As I sat gazing idly one day
My reflection, sky clouds and sun
In Mottled leafy greenish stream
A gunshot came from somewhere
Then silence did resume
With a sharp breath of Grief

Problem's of a Past and Present Future

Love's gentle honesty—lost for too long a time
       As a Lover fell to the shadows
       Gasping in the drought of laughter
          And tears

A sometimes silent tomb

Shadow Boxing his Past
       In a box

A Slave—In relentless memory

Solitudes brutality—became itself alive and wise
       To the gruesome eyes shaped like gallows
       Severance Letching in the face of Hallowed
          Fears

These now blackened wounds

Scarves circling this skull
       In swirls

To pages—Rags of rage in story

Sleeping selfish vanities—Hidden and long since denied
       Both in action and action supplied now
       Energy, passion and duty to endeavor
          The Years

The Lover lost forever in circling moons

Rising tides of Lust
              In action
              In ages

Trapped In no man's glory

Regenesis

E genesis Mort
       Genesis
E Genesis incorped
       Y Genesis
E la Genesis
       Regenesis
Il a Fa
       Mi
Un Genesis
       Eteus I Et

So?—Another Poem eh?

Which is its coincidental title,
Then I junked it up for weeks
This poem doesn't rhyme I thought I said
And then all we had was so

I'll make this one rhyme, hmm
Another poem eh?—I drank the dreams
Poured prophecies too pleasant and sweet—since
Which the air grew to taste bitter

Everyone's sense, especially mine
Found to much reason this time
To waste words on meaningless rhymes
Too dream was—perchance to try and fly
Away, Too, From, And For, and Dance Divine

The stagnant fool soon did rot away

Do you Dance?

Succubus and her form

Her piercing steel eyes of my demise
As she scorched holes in the back of my skull
Now ceiling tiles in a disused
Burnt out factory

Noises in my mind drown and reprise
Again they gurgledrunkening bell tolls
Chimes of rhymes inanity
Fused sanity's story

Deaths grinning rotted teeth between thighs
Her eyes swivel and writhe no flow control
Drowning the beast
Eye's burning glory

Words of poison venom masked disguise
Claps of traps trappings and spiked pitfall holes
The last warmth found trickling
Bloods lustful history

I saw her mind melt stranger arise
With a sunrise drowning moons satyrs and foals
Gentle lamb of a nighttimes dream
Now in beastly fury

Licking her teeth lips and smile I die
Knees three feet beneath the ground I scowl
Horned Howls chocking on salted earth
Soaked in fluid

Remnant shards of that broken night
Still swirl this scarred heart

Telling fortunes/ artificial lights

I cannot be sure In my self, moments or
                    Future—For the lights has
                    Gone—they have left me
                    In darkness
I cannot bear their absence in those lights
                    Visions—Instincts in the darkness has
                    Grown—and has bought with
                    It Doubt
I do not believe in fortunes in itself, telling or
                    Minds eyes—for the lights may have
                    Known—and in trickery only
                    Artificial
I believe the light of day might be explained though by
]   Whom—I do not know

I believe in my birth I believe in my death
And everything between will surely
Only just ride with me.

The Balance

I love honesty
Only if it's Cryptic

I'm a repressed Trauma
       Trapped in a Train Station

Got to Get to a Bridge

       A real one
              That's not Burning
       This Time

That's when it got obvious

       When it became
              Non—Representational
       When it became
              Imageless

I could see it more clearly

Then the Honesty
       Worked through the Trauma
       Into Silence
              And Clarity

The Birth

The nine muses—glorious
Daughters of Hera

Some devious, others Angelis
Swept me away In
Another dream—the debris
Alone it stayed behind
To testify its time
Eratio led my final choir
As if God's Gabriella
　　　　Herself
Though the song remains
　　　　Alone

The Coma's

I laid my life to death
        In five different dreams
Concurrent
        Interweaving dispersing
        Themselves
                Plot thickening
        Disease ridden things
The First I dream't five years
        In a deep unconscious similar to a coma
Awoke in a chair;
        The left half of my face in Shreds
                And drunk upon waking
                Twice as suicidal
Seventeen—and sure of my death
        Before I was Twenty Three
It gave me a psychosis
        And after two years its phenomenology
                Overwhelmed me
Building a dreamlike existence of nightmares
        This led to a compilation of nightmares
I called "The tale of a Poet"
A Happy Luckless charmer
        Who noticed five alternatives to
        The underpinning truths of a
                Reality
Schizophrenic, delusions and voices—dreams
                And Déjà vu
        Forced me into counseling and therapy
Whence I began to rewrite the attempt
        An accurate Psychological Horror

Desperate for a cure outside of
Drugs
       Cognitive design, Psychodynamic analysis
       And non representational Jungian Archetypes
I called it "All along the watchtower"
       How longs an elastic band?
            Its infinite its concept
            But merely the
Weight of its design
Is Infinity
       Of any weight—In its design
Then philosophically
       Washed away reality itself
       As a Double headed Spoon

The death of a memory

In the darkest dream I've enjoyed in these passing months
The dampening of my joy throughout these days
Being brutal and ceaselessly tiring
I came across her once more, and one last time

Thinking time had changed me or I with time proved me a fool
An arrant knave to return just As I had been before
'cept brutally and ceaselessly tired
She mouthed some concerns, Soundless but important

Skipping reels of the horrors in my mind were still all
I had to offer along with a self-centered sense of their reality
One brutal and ceaselessly tiring
I knew to set her free, from the tyranny of my company

And waking ashamed, almost new—after reliving that final
departure
Trapped in that same sordid state chiming in with that forelorn
fate
Old and Tired
She lingered softly, the image of my Madonna

Fading through the darkness into shadows—that place
Where all is forgotten eventually off in hiding
Only to echo its once prominent existence

I felt that breath that comes with death
The death of a memory
My meandering Madonna.

The Divine Muse

In a dream—
I was deceived by the arrival
                    Of a Muse
In a Meadow,
Lonely long and tired; a mist
                    Gently settling
            Beneath a solitary Bold and Majestic
                    Oak

Sat a gentle looking raven haired girl
            Of Seventeen
            Slightly Freckled
                    With sensuous green eyes
            Of Marble
                    Colored as
                            The Earth Itself
Her Aura, Green and Silver
            Seemed to take the darkness
                    Onto itself,
                            Deepening like
                            The Cosmos
                                    Itself

She said that she was hidden
            Lost along a Journey
                    But she had yet to arrive
Your eyes I cried—I feel as though
            They've seen me
                    For the first time
            I've ever been seen

And she whispered
            That her Eyes Had saved her
Father Once
            And that he was a dreamer too

40

The Fable of Faith Falter
And
"Ashtray Jazz"

Deep, almost hid and completely surrounded in the catacombs
of an artists studio
Sat smoke with his fingers light against the sheer vacuum of his
inner demon soul
With Faith and her company both shining and new willing to
love and in love with willing
While riddle played a banjo, and whittled the hope he hoped
would finally stop faith faltering
Whilst faltering alone knew only herself and how she had
once been a plaything for faith
Fire, he was in meditation, and stasis preparing to burn when
the fuel was already a flame
And Hope was dancing to the waves of the ride, which tilted
and turned like rips in a tide
Matchstick was near, he held for three things, to keep dear for
a while for when time was awry
Transience she asked where's the other side, I got to move on
to save a life
And Riddle sat crossed legged and hummed, to a sitar and
Arabian drum, in a d that droned
Zippo played like a candelabra flickering through idea's and
igniting them in his passions
While Lane, spun her yarns to his ever loving ears, wandering
in and out of his dreams
And Ashtray came through with a Jazz trumpet and a
concoction of blue rhythmic notes
And Rain she burst into flames—and danced wildly with her
new and everlasting sauvignon
Dressing now these days as an expensive French cigarillo with
gold lettering above the stub and a scent within the paper

The Last Letter

The Very last letter After I learn't
        Of her bittersweet tainted Revenge
        Against the smallest of my
        Attempts—To Love

I returned to my penned
        Grave—a humble corpse
        Groom of no matched
            Unkemptness
        My Poverty stricken self
        Forsaken by a monstrous
            Whore of a saint
            Made Brutal
        In Petty Jealousies

Could I measure—Beauty
In this new Solitude
Like a Setting
        Burnt out
            Sun

The Leaves

Years Before——When the sun shone brighter for me
   Than these stars and moon
I was swallowed in and gathered up

Between the breezes, Love sang with me

Years Before——In the last autumn that truly burst
   Before the black began to bleed
I was using up the last of my warmth on her

In frozen years, soon to follow——too iced over to Rot

Years Before——Unaware in the bliss of her arms
   That I would never force her to stay
I was lost in a last chance——She was soon to wander

Sinking Hearts in bloodied seas

  Too Numb to Swim

    Too dead and heavy to float

      Too Deep a Sea——Baron Abyss

Endlessly, Effortlessly

   Swallowed in and Gathered up.

The Mistress

Love is a mistress
Who has spurned me
For the very price
Of love
That she knows I refuse to pay

Who gave me a lenient sentence
And I was sentenced
To Just sex
And the Rain
The Only dream I awoke into

Ravaged Rooms, Carnage and Death
     Scarred, broken Jawed and Blind
     The truth came with knives
         And Cried—You Hath
]   Betrayed all of my
            Theft—Did
            I Steal
            Your soul?
         Or something more
To which I fell in no pity
     To the floor
     And cried
         My body My body
         Knows no mind

     Nor does it vainly
         Celebrate
         A soul

The Psychobabble of love

Don't lie to me!—I'd be lying if I said I didn't lie—that's the
truth, honestly—Ask any of my friends, but watch out, their not
as honest with you as I am

She drew sharp breaths—the last to turn and leave were her
eyes.
I was dragged into the forum, but I was already a spectacle
The balls in her court, always was, always will be

We see you more as a writer?—Why! Are these writers hands,
if they are I'll carve them anew for you—though nothing
knows what you want. Did I fall too quick? Or was I stumbling
into a ravine.

She told me to look her in the eyes—I gave a stare, but it was
ineffective
Never in a room alone again—just biased witnesses
We should fill the world up with literal poems—where hearts
aren't allowed to be fiery

Sarcasm again, eh?—Only on Wednesdays unless its
Thursday, but I'm always too late. I was too late for my own
life once, but I heard it was awful. I knew a bullet dodger

She had me on my knees once—she'll have it again soon—A
ring made from this broken band
A wandering mutual friend, pointedly knew—I thought I was
busy
The band that strangles this fluttering bird in the bird's nest tis
not mine to break

The twenty thousand Tuesdays

I'd heard the birds still gather
                Around that bench
A pecking order of love, luck and lust
        Where mine
              Was laid to rest

Twenty thousand Tuesdays
        Passing now
            Like death

I'd pecked my cage since forever
Began to retch
A hungry ashtray drowning deep in dust
        Reward
            Promised in flesh
Two tragic Tuesdays
        Spent cold
            With baited breath

I'd spite my night a feather
              Without a breast
A parapet of tar grown in gaps of gust
        Bald wings
            Torn by the Mesh
The twenty thousand Tuesdays
        Cancelled
            By bad health

The Two Insomniacs

After Three years of a night time madness
Each night a Wild flight
        Desperately trying to escape
          My Dreams
My Sub-conscious finally snapped
        And forced its way into my
          Awoken Life

And Found a Book I had carelessly written and left
        Upon a shelf
        Called "All along the watchtower"
—Shakespearian—about a Dream
            Inside a Dream
        About A Dream

Based on a song
By Bob Dylan

Thirty-Three Chapters
        Made of dream's and
          Short stories
Allegorical of most things

        But strictly so of my
        Memories
            And Life
A Haunting tale of Lucidity
        Inside a dreamt Trap
Built from my own
Psychology

And Never A Destination

There's Just a letter Left

The Letter I had sent—Torn and Crumpled
　　　　After suffering the abuse
　　　　　　　Of my frustrations

Choking over words as they were
　　　　Laid then Lost
　　　　　　　The language absconding
　　　　　　　　From sense
　　　　Deviating in useless terms

Loves Intention—Coming off the page
　　　　　　　As scathing statements
　　　　　　　　Of self Neglect

I knew the letter could never be read
On inspections—
The revelations of my love—
　　　　Just Dead foam streaming
　　　　　　　Instead of the tear's
That were long since Dead

The letter was re-written—The New
　　　　One read better though
Any of sense of self
　　　　　　　Was spared

The Letter then was sent——With No reply
      For Years
            Alone and deadened

      Too weak to struggle

            With the letter that
              Was Left

Three's and believers

I'll be there—someone—whom?

And the drums I cannot mend
A loss of the dream's
That were not mine

Yours in feign design
For purposes

This presence is a present

Precious Palpitation

Three's and believers
Trapped through and around
Did you ever?

Sometimes I wonder

Totem Poles

For the Garden—Bird chimes toll
For the Garden—Small mammals burrow holes
For the Garden—The blue sky with sunshine glow
For the Garden—we bought some decorative totem poles

In the Garden—I smoked a fresh ciggerette
In the Garden—The ripened tomatoes looked wet
In the Garden—The gate was buckled and bent
In the Garden—The totem poles made my lover upset

Now the Garden—Generally well kept
Now the Garden—flowers healthy none inept
Now the Garden—watered, no thirst or death
Now the Garden—Totem pole where shadows are kept

The school of fools—No ships

Well this school of fools, with their Big Ideas
Has shut down now, for the next few years
Taught the Kids well, To Hunt down their Fears
And I just stood around grinning

Then the prince of fools, he asked me what's my game
I said "sorry son, but what's your name"
He said "I'll kill you, if you cheek me again"
And I couldn't breathe for the laughter

Now the innocent town, was over run by thieves
The Beggar's stared, questioning their beliefs
The guards said "whoa lads, please keep this brief"
And I just walked away smiling

Well the drunk disciples, of this new regime
lost themselves and said, "what does this mean"
The Hero said "not now, I'm still trying to get clean"
And I said "you've led them blindly to slaughter"

The Hero said "you know man, I think your right
Come and be my doctor, I could spare your life"
He said, "Do I look like I sleep at night"
And I said "No man you look like your dying"

He said "watch out, deaths only for the weak"
I threw away my faith, there's truth in his speech
He caught my eye, and said "beware those who teach"
And I said "You couldn't teach me if you wanted to"

Well I found the Doctor, with Gin on his breath
He screamed to me "save me, from all of this death"
I said "calm down now, there's no-one left"
And he said "at least your an angel for trying"

Silent intensity . . . . Tempered insanity . . . . Argued reality . . . . Trapped internally

Lost outside of your own true mystery, false faces search your own constantly, attacking all of your honesty, feeding at the feet of your dignity.

Lustful Lover kept hidden to shameful secrecy, comes once with writhing passion to question all their decency, kept locked in vacant vacuum to vacate all useless scrutiny, Chained Shackled and torn from all who come to please him

He lies behind such ruthless eyes and makes such pretty mask, His voice so new yet screams of truth and dances to all that's asked, with answer bold and often cold scripted lifetimes in advance, it begs belief that joker or could thief play role to which he wants

He wants what's never been known by him before, the illusion that evades him like jealous whore, the sin denied him since from peace he was torn, caught well beyond the cheap freedom he adorns

The lustful eyes that dream and dream only, look beyond prized trinkets and costume jewellery, search past pretence and burdened society, keep intrigued glimpse of innocence and shameless foolery

To touch taste and relish in utter purity

When she would sing

I used to write poems, in days spent alone
In smokey, dank basement public houses

The atmospheres bliss echoed stronger with beating
Silence, hmm's and brr's, mechanical Orchestra's

I'd write an Ode to the silence—for the nothingness or
A Sonnet only I would witness, 'cept for the barmaid

      Who knew me well

I was sure of our love, Vows of silence—She shared
With me the lighting of a candle

Through days and weeks, months and seasons, each day
Reasons grew stronger to return

I was sure the silence would shatter breaking gates for
the thousand wishes that

      Now bound us before we had begun

On the chilliest Morn of the turning into spring
  As the last frost resolved itself a dew
    I sang a song of victory before the bolted door
      Humming a tune of love both inevitable and won

With an Audacious "Already" Attitude
      I strode into
Burning Caverns of desire
      To find that she was gone

A SERIES OF MASKS

Portraiture/Caricature

Condors, Griffins, Circling Vultures,
The Dancing shadows beneath—Grotesque
Silhouettes of gross natures, caricatures—

Glinting among them the torn war suits of horses
Heaped in an embrace—Morbid figures—
Among the cavaliers mangled corpses

Dry set, as if Oil on canvas—Picturesque
The still setting in serene portraiture
The passing battle bloody by request

Pecking orders squabble in rackets
To test the stench—the baked rotting flesh
Under a sun crying—writhing with cosmic ratchets

The feasting churning in frenzied gorging
Once the roosts aligned and at rest
With the dueling and lurid taunting

Between sharpened claws
And blunted
Hooves
The March
The feast
The land shall
Scavenge
Its fill

Of personality
And Paint

An Imitation

A mirror—A Measure—Contact—Equal
Against sense—To conjure something unreal
Attract an imitation—An Azreal

Tongues and eyes grow wildly to testify
Growing dangers—Lost chance to rectify
This grievous fault—Jekyll; Nullify

Transmogrify—The joke seems banal
As a source loses favor to the Gall;
A fleshy clown—growing clever and bold

Vicious cycles Eyes flash colors of Ruth
Blood Reds and pale ghost whites—Vacuous, Sparse
As the sanity diminishes—Stalls

The rolling years—Too busy to recall
The depths of fabrication to the farce
Too long this disguise becoming foolproof

The eyes cannot believe an unseen truth

           The Image—Connections Severed
                The eventual suicide
                     Numb
                              And Meaningless
                The price of pride
                     In a reckless Mr. Hyde

"Manicism"

From the tree, and the seen—branches of the dead,
Leaves—The perfect unique patterns of lives been,
The gnarled bark makes masks—Tracks of fate left spent

Inner veins flow energies of life and growth
To reach skies and heavens in times maudlin march
The seed—Born in a drunken mysticism

Unpregnant of thy cause—to impregnation

In the deep drowning sensation—Conscience—
Arrives—Great Jupiter's Universal Joke
Over shadowed by limp kookaburra's

With three second memories of three short years—
The squalid state of thoughts transgressions
Inane—Damned delirium—Manicisms

Suffering as a consequence
The seeds relentless
Reincarnations

As flowers
Birds
Dews and dawns

Bone Structure

Gazing—Into Space—Burst—Imagination
Conjures Visions—Majestic Genus Corvus
Androgynous—An immaculate creation

Its dark Attire set against a nimbus
A sky threatening to tear itself apart—To shatter
Into an eternal darkness—Erebus

And other Protogenoi preparing for her;
This devil noir angelica—bird of prey
To signal a shift—for this event to spur

The nimbus swells and consumes the last of grey
Leaving a trace, a silver silhouette—Brazen
her head jerks, feathers flare—Along the causeway

To the field—In flight—doomed as storms hasten
Winds flail her to the ground, bones splinter—Fracture
Beaten into Rocks—Her majesty stolen

The waves crash putting salt to wounds—Rupture
To ligaments and flesh—Against gravity
She climbs upright—damaging perfect structure

Spine, Shoulder and withered wing—Deformity
Disaster—Such tragedy in conception
Pricelessly over consumed in vanity

The Empty space—Now—Too full of Destruction

Death

Presuming a humble mortality
A pristine, perfectly wide harrowing grin
Seem less image—Picturesque vitality

Into this adornment—Purely reflection;
A haunting of deaths grim visage—plays disguise
To learn itself—in a heartbeats perfection

Within earthly skin, bursts and grows—festers
Ancient—from within mocks this mask—Artifact
To its honesty—Artifice sequesters

Broken—to its delible plasticity
Its shine, vibrance, beauty—Reduced to sin
Panic erupts—Pseudo-serendipity
                                        Shatters

Blood stained bruises—Patterned Genus Nester's
Painted below—under glow and health of skin
The tortured eternal stench of deaths specters

Rising—bringing with it—to the illusion
Its character—grotesque, limp, lifeless—Abstract
A sensory depth—A phantom allusion

Death itself aware—As man's inheritance
In nature, present, constant; a legal writ
In contract—Nor nullified for brilliance

The Mask—breaking to fragility—to ruin

Its Naivety lost against its demise
                                        To Tatters

The Exposed Soul

Precious passeridea—A domestic sparrow
Tamed over time—still, transfixed—whistling prophecies
To the rain—beyond the narrow gap of the window

In Thunder and crashing lightning—gentle harmonies
From derelict cage, an abandoned room—an echo
Songs of a lost freedom—twelve forgotten symphonies

The bird in hand—pale thin—Caught with wing clips
Bruised—Placed bait for a reptilian menagerie
Never Nursed—Just perched above juniper and tulips

Once brilliant and wild—Tropical, Javanese
Poised; keeping appetites blood thirsty—forked tongues, lips
Perhaps in a fable befitting of Sophocles

A proud Mother—Once—Now childless and a widow

Sunken Eye

Rumors of lost scrolls—far off hermit Towers
—Artist, philosopher, scholar, alchemist
Beyond moats, mountains—the coastline and showers

The Hermit—long tired; he and his prominent wist
Defeated by time and age—wilting flowers
Countless passing seasons—A sandglass just twists

Turns—As it empties—the damp glow turns sapphire
Through the dust—made of the purest amethyst
Upon works of this once respected friar

Tattered pages; Experimental powers
Medicines, Algebra's—A broken desire
The best kept—In pressed envelopes—Love Letters

The beating hearts of poems of youthful Trysts

In Shields of Moonbeams
        The branches Shadows
Sight—Stalks
        The dense overgrowth

For Prey
        To betray

        The safety of its slumber

Carnage/Desire

A lust that's swallowed prepares to rage
A cause for curses to swirl and burn
Fuelled—ferment as spirits with age

To poison minds and the heart that yearns
Into decay corrode, corrupt
Its breath and stench in boiling guts turn

Sickening the feeling to quell, quash
Stifle and silence, A petty price
For an honesty lost soon to wash;

In its own colors, then to congeal
Tainted, thick and ugly to hatred
Spite and self loathing—raised as Veal

Alone and poorly nursed—Mistreated
The soul planning refuge till release
The Lust in strengths revenge defeated

Began reasoning's began Damage
Before instances before Desire
Over sacrifice over Carnage

        The self destruction
                The Phoenix of Love
        A heart
           Attempts to Grow
                From the Ashes

FLY BY NIGHT

Number 1

I'm sorry
          Do you lick your teeth?
If only sometimes

I'm sorry again
          Why can't I breathe?
If only sometimes

I'm just sorry
          That's as far as it go's
Sometimes again

I cried sorry
          Without the tears though
This time
Many many sometimes Again

Number 2

I gave both thanks and wishes and dreams into the only arms that knew some truth.
I gave secrets all three of both of them to eyes that met only mine—pure and free. In an office torn down and I remember burning.
I gave the few gifts I was saving from them selves in a moonlit ceremony, away from where they grew in zealous Jest.
I gave inane and confused the jealousy you bought and used to poison my mind, reserving spite for he who was poisoned.
I gave no signs or posts, directions or maps. I had none to give I and others saw.
I gave scars and marred the man who betrayed you with his doubt and silence—you gave a laugh and it taught me well.
I gave complete nothingness, I gaze and gawk and gape at the pretty misfortune, my mirrored madness, making messy use of misery.
I gave as good as I got which is less to say how much I was given, but more to which I could muster—smiles and miles I could not travel that bridge that burnt between us.
I gave the smirks from a jerk, Tears born from jeers the hope of jokes and another from nowhere—you gave me a shameful insight into all I could never be or have.
I gave hollow hounds their howls in a fireless night peeling shades from the moon ad scratching to the silver I'd been promised—losing fingernails.

I gave in to the truth—That I could never, despite myself, forsaking all others—pretending the self.

And the silence is a Fish Tank.

The damsel and the dark

Throw a rope, I'll make my ascent
     Fag in mouth
Unkempt, A Ragged Romeo in rags
Skuff my trainers along the brickwork
Graze a knee on a loose ledging
Attain a scar from a rogue nail
     We'll laugh about it later
  For Now
    Throw me a rope

At the top, I'll stake a claim
     And new route
Fresh Breath, Casanova back from the dregs
Untie my tongue with a melody
Sing so soft, A lover's whisper,
Resound, a pennywhistle verse
     We'll sing it again later
  For Now
    Throw me a rope

Near the dawn, I'll guide your descent
                Fag in mouth
Piquet, Jongleur—Jumping Jack in a bag
Bargain with a gamblers pride, one bet
Love being for an after party
Echo, As wounds and flesh regale
                Repaid too much too later
        And Now
                Into the dawn

On the ground, disguised in vain
                Destitute
Redempt, Chaos—her charms, wits, badge and tags
Depart, but she beckons a return.
Her lingering scent, sultry tone
Plays a symphony, swift and terse
                Reverbs long into later
        Now And
                Into the dawn

With the breeze, and sparrow accent
Fag in mouth
Now deaf, Nyx—her raven hair pressed with pegs
Returns, to kiss the day a good night
As I, in wanderlusts stupor
Follow a gaze for direction
Steps to be traced much later
Now free
Swept, like a breeze

In a song, A new refrain
A flash flute
Ricochet, Erebus—gifted his dog tag
To burn, in chosen ceremonies
With love, poses, advocacy.
Into this crime I fell alone
Truth's veil slipped much later
Free, now
Swept, with a breeze

A POETS PSYCHOSIS

Via Absurdity alone

This room's a cage—A popular scream
    Complaint or observation
From within the cage
Outside the room is a house—It's a cage
     Within another cage
  The house is made of cages
     Or room's
The house is one of millions
   That's cage—To the power of a million
    It's a quantifiable concept

Gather the houses—draw imaginary
  Boundaries
    Hallucinate an excuse
A cage by extension
  Then extension
    And more extension

The cage is now so big and brave
  It's existential in
Nature

Then the cage is merely within
The caged

A Collection of choices

I'd like a straightjacket please
Priceless Poetica
        Pristine Poison
I'm getting skeptical
        About Death again
He turned up in a dream
        And said
                Choose a game
I chose the game of life
        I've been losing ever
                Since

But I stole his knowledge of
        Dreams

Escaped
And never came back

Till the Straight Jacket
        Arrived

A Meander

This nightmared endeavor
   Each Solid burst into this realm
I shaped in colours from a dark drawing
   Etched imprints—Under Eyelids
Each another other form of the infinite times
   Ripped asunder—
Torn into bits
A circle of Hell
   With personal design

I know myself to be catered for

I—A Hound at a teet

A Bare bitches poisoned Breast

Feasted
   Fattenned
     Soon to Suckle
My Mocking Misery

A Noteless Suicide
Duly Noted

I'm going down—To the places
        Where my thoughts tend to drown

With a pair of Iron lungs

        An infamous disappearance

Noting a notorious noteless suicide
        Duly noted

I'm drowning shapes—In the places
        Where death's twice the impossibility of escape

With a dozen torn tongues

        And drunken endurance

Noting a notorious noteless suicide
        Duly noted

I'm sinking ships—In the places
        Where sails were already made of flames

With pain, burning numb

        Baron clearance

Noting a notorious noteless suicide
        Duly noted

Washing Machine

I came across the Tundra,
        Lost against
                A measured silence
As I created the darkened
        Spot lit stages
                For my dreams once
                        More
The earlier shows
        And seasons of strange
                Faces,
                        Spectators
Now all I miss
        That Mirrored edge
                Of despair
        Upon which
        I wish only now
                To be

        Eternally Twinned
                And Pinned

Admonition

Admonition, Volition on a shrieking viola
        Get as awake as you can be
Be more bolder in the tombola

Joke bets in this time tunnel casino
        Will be met with
                Forcible Ejection

Admittance, remembrance in a summer shack
        Be there for her and the breeze
Get the folder in the blue black bag sack

Misprints in this psychological block
        Will be drafted
                Pending Rejection

Anarchy, Apathy to a flagged Page
        Get all the gist's to freeze
Be beholder of a free life stage

Misfire's in the epiphany gallery
        Will be redrawn
                Quoted on inspection

Animated, Autonomy felt like new jeans
        Be the tomb and matt chrome Key
Get much older, begin the gangrene scene

Joke hearts in the azure universe
        Will be reclaimed
                Quo-gratis Retention

An Allegory of the mind

Be fair—and leave them all alone
        Now—Forever

Torture just me
                Mind

Give me back
        My green eyes
The devil's blue eyes
        I cannot
        Love her

My green eyes alone
Are more priceless

An allegory of the Mind

My mind is a mangled backward lathe that takes
Inventions and dismantles them to their
Components
A factory and architectural studio that
Redesigns all entry input to remanufacture
Innovations—At the risk of destruction
And the promise of invention
Never Pretension

My minds a broken toy acting out against its
Owner for being callous and careless—
Complaints
A sandbox and nursery for
Pedestrian thoughts to speed along
With an edge made of space time
Dynamics—At the risk of destruction
And the promise of invention
Never Retention

My minds a mind made like all others a miser
To mistakes and a greenish envy to success or
Restraints
An animal whose hunger is for meaning
Aberrance and the work of conceptual
Practice—At the risk of destruction
And the promise of Invention
Never Ever
Paying Attention

An Attempt

An attempt at tranquil peace, A refuge
A more solid silence to the design
Escaping a distance measured by minds
And locking in a box its subterfuge
An attempt to beguile framed woodworks
To contain the stillness the silence brings
The humming of hummingbird machines sings
Before the dampening of the dam with words smirks
An Attempt at all other forms of space
No track or trace, rhyme or pace—just bleached walls
With salt scented air, chateau, gusts and gall's
The settings in the grace of setting pace
An attempt before there's nothing else left
Or else than everything there, just to muse
That thought and motion was all to refuse
The element of this rogue prince of theft
The thief of time
      In Rhymes and Chimes
        Alone

Characters

I've created Comparisons
        And contrasts
        Only characters
                Against characters

In definition of life itself,

        I es; E, us
            I
It's Inadequate
Teaching myself how to fish

        Just had all my fishes
Stolen
        By Bigger Fish

What an Adventure!

Cold Coffee

I need a bucket and spade
        To collect the overwhelming joy
Erupting from this void
        "Its in Kilo's and Seconds
            Heavy moments
Lighter shades of disruption"—

        In-between these blank stares
The gold strewn across the canvas looks
        Expensive—I've taught myself to be
            Tasteless—With a mistake I
              Learnt long ago

The imagery found through this cup of
        Cold coffee
Looks like more Cold coffee

And I begin to pray—that my souls lethargy
        Musters strength
            To keep emptying my Bucket

Danse Macabre

Apresvousmonami
          Mes companion Solitaire
Ma   Savoir saint
Dansmonjoue—Le mid-nuitheure

C'etaituntrajedy un horrifique

Jonchees de debris, commesisa
                    Propremisere

Folie de uneboissonsucree a

Je me nois, pour sauvegarder
cettehomme qui se noire

Garcon Glasse
Dansmonglasse
Dans le mid-nuitheure

Mon fragile jeu de

Et un

Dans Macabre

I was never given the truth

I remember once three years ago too soon from
Now that there was a truth and a cause for
The condition I have become and personified.
Now in a psyche ward—after a suicide attempt
The reward offered as well that I never saw or met
Or even made sure of—by no word or warning
Was I suspected to believe the possibility?
Imagined scenario or reject the principles of my
own imagined self
—I remember the length and immaculate design
The perfection to his creation
I even foresaw his inevitable defeat and
Destruction
I guess now—he was built to be destroyed

Three years now with nothing to show but a
Personal growth—a realization that there
Was no truth but merely a promise I
Took the suicide and its attempt—the Violators
Now with nothing to gain from me with
A soul so abandoned and sentenced to
Hell or maybe a beautiful forgiveness just hurt
To have my mind body and soul put up for
Free as toys with no reward
—Still on this other side of it all I do
Admit to very little regrets but more
A sorrowful admittance to all the
Millions of mistakes this makeshift
Jekyll made in his stride

Invisible scars

This room—covered, littered
    In spited words
            Invisible scars

Carved, embedded on walls
        Mirrored surfaces
Black like bile—on a map

A universal mistake
        An epicenter of Folly
A centrifugal player
        Plucking pity
            For a price

Life was a theater—A grandiose
        Event—Ancient, New
            And Dying
In its essence of Living
        Trapped in these terms
Though never denied
        Itself for the sake
            Of its forsaken
                Self

I, now smoke
        Dancing a melody

Jagged Edges

Jagged, Jarred—Sold and scarred

Breaking dogs, teeth, bone
        And trampling through
             The Marred
Barricaded bookshelf

The gaunt saddled savior

Slipping chains, Reigns and the rain
And laying near
The lure
A lock of feathered hair

Hung, Hurled—Sung and swirled

Tearing Rags, Masks, Thrones
And swallowing
            The burns
Phoenix flames and ashtrays

The pyre, webbed wings

Ragged flames, frames and pains
        And smoking breezes
            The style
                Turns

An Escapist stare's unknown
        Deeper into the Cosmos
            Of a night sky

Litany

In a Fire—Blazing strong—Even against
                    The Relentless Bitter Cold
            The Muddied Dirty Snow

An Ancient Magic Found me
With My Guitar—Solitarily Singing

The Night and its Silence
                    Deep and Eternal
            Where a Shadow's Stretch
                    And Reach is Limitless

Spirit's of Wolves and Nymphs
                    Satyrs
            Erupted from the smoke
                    And in Flight
            Entertained me as I sang

I Spent hours as they—In Birth
            Mystified me in Dance
        To then
                Upon impact of the
            Low hanging Branches

            Disappear—Leaving Eyes

Green like Leaves
        Red like Fire
                And Blue like Ice

The Song sweeping away September

        In a Magic of its own

The strangest memory of now

This geometry—circles symmetry
Phantom Puppetry
And the such
Too, Too much

Under Scrutiny
The makings of Mutiny

An Orb—In a crystal Ball

Past and Present Haunting
Each other in turn
From a future I forgot
Long ago

No choice this time
Around

The attempt to flee
A déjà vu dream
An element of itself

Is it written in the fabric?
To sense the
Manufactured
Tragic
Fractured
Panic

Philosophies on Ghosts

God forbid my soul
      This endeavor be so cruel
That I am permitted to enter it
at all
      Let a life be truer too
      That I should do it alone

A Denial—would leave me damned
And damnation alone
        Breeds bad Ghosts

I am not bred in the same
      Manner as ghosts
Nor in the curiosities
      Of similar likeness
      Of Ghost seeking
        Individuals

The truest sense of death
      Then Belongs
Where it can be relied
      Upon the most
In Graves,
      Memories
      And Man made myths

Placeboes

Cursed further, every moment, every beat
Dragging still, by boot heels, through this street
My neck sore, my knee's weak
My spine crunches, cracks, tweaks

Lamplight glow, dim lit grey, every fifteen feet
Trotting speed, still diseased, trying not to speak
An overflow, words of soul—formed just to dispose
And be disposed and closer now

Looking glass, looking fast, drenched in gasoline
Match on fire, burning desire, smoking dreams
Soulless eyes—gleam in silent screams
Living the impossible, kind of how it sounds

On my thirty third cigarette—I came to calm
And with the trickling specks of Gin hitting throat
I grew numb—The blade locked well away
Placebo, Placebo
        Each scar—Placebo

Now—Still never really free

        Just Placeboes
            To keep me off of
                The Placeboes

Plans Permissions and some coded language

Prayers

       Proverbs and Poetries

Insanity

       Personified building

       Up a reality—shaped in

       Jerked movements—control zones

       Flattering—Any fool of humanity

       That occurred—

       If she drives here

       Again—to sneak herself

       A nothingness—She Just hates

The Darker Glints in my Eyes

I'm being Haunted
        Viciously by women
Its not
        A Vicious haunting
The women
        Are not Vicious
Though I'm left
        Feeling haunted
Viciously
        By women
Often not
        Viciously enough

You'll catch them sometimes
        In my Eyes
        Glinting

The escape routes

En embandenment
>   This memory went nowhere
>   Again
>   This bottle's not bottomless
>   Again
I am in a refrain—Again
As the escape routes—used themselves
>   For themselves

En embitterment
>   These theories go nowhere
>   Again
>   And Again
>   The can and hands in unison
>   Again
>   And Again
I am in a refrain—Again and Again
As the escape routes—Stole themselves
>   For themselves

En entertainment
>   These jokes hold no hope
>   Yet Again
>   The laughter's under the weight
Of being strangled
I am in a refrain—once again
As the escape routes—still themselves
>   For themselves

Leaving me behind
>   Again

The Eye

I imagine myself at all times
      A very lucky disposable
Camera
      The Photograph
Imagery built and built again

Till my imagination floods
      Streaming
      Film after Film

      Dreamt Rewards

The Damnation came
      As image itself
Grew wise
      Bold
        And quick

Disrupting the pace of
my sleep

Does a nightmare
      Love
It's relentless
      Reincarnation
When I lost my love
      For Sleep

The Factory

The Rota
      I've got a second hand dependency
For Time

Mental Crawl Spaces

Tryclic—Motor Neurone
      Synapse
    Constant Recall
        Physical Muscle
          Memory

Bio—Rhythmic
    Cycles
    Pattern Determination
      Concretion
      Fixation

Ritualism
    Dependency And
Repeat

The Fiery Furnace of Fancy Fliers

Infinity began to burn in a crimson flame that tore my eyes
through time
Through the darkness of my iris into the caverns of the self
Possibility multiplied with itself and over again

The beast danced wildly till the muscles burned as the flames
around his hollow halo
A false cheap glimmer of gold licking edges of the razored flames
Damnation multiplied with itself and over again

The Goddess came to make my case with tongues of a
thousand truths
And taught me my shame taking me away from the trial and
revelation
Salvation multiplied with itself and over again

I was scarred—my soul lay invisibly torn and ripped beneath
sullen skin and
Sunken flesh—An eternal pain never to be seen by eyes and minds
Dejection multiplied with itself over and over again

In the places of holy worship I stood before the name higher
than the name
Preparing a prayer for mercy, and a reverence for the prayer
A blessing in guise,
Multiplied with itself
Over and Over again
Amen

The Grass Grown

I've killed myself in
       Too many dreams
          This time
              Why?
There are no moments in oblivion
       No other side

This loss now made
       Gentle against eternity
       An Interruption
       Would be a meaningless
          Blade of Graa
          Knives of
              The sea
  Or
       Scythes
          In The
          Harvest
This old world, I have fallen into
       The only judge being
          Eventualities edge

Life's too much chaos
       To ever be caught

Where's this Happy Ending

It's buckled under the heat of stress
A mess, I confessed—getting undressed
Under duress
    In the beggar's best

It's escaped with the rest
From its hidden chest

A diamond bay and cove
    Let's Jest

It's rancid now and depressed

    Repressed

And a quest, an excuse for a test
Expressed, though less
    Than the mess
I do confess
    The duress

The secretest
    Incompletest
        Defeatist
    In a heat of stress

The Lost Romantic

I would swim a thousand stroked a million times, and back and
forth
Kept afloat by your vision and leaving trails of dreams
In an oceans current
Of your wisest direction

I would lock away jealousy, chain up pettiness drown the
notions of doubt
In buckets of rain gather the wilderness and lay it
At the ceremony, basking in the glow
Of your wisest direction

I would travel North to howl down the icy winds, fired inside
by your image
Cold and ice thawed away as I burn, fuelled by the
Love beauty and honor
Of your wisest direction

I would dance filthy wet and drowning too, in the rains of all
your tears
Flood my swollen lungs threatening my own death to bring you
Hope laughter joys and smiles
To your wisest direction

I would swallow words to sour or sweet to make your air
cringe in falsehood
My honesty brutal and fair is all I can promise though my mind
wanders
I gather tie and bind myself
To your wisest direction

I in and around consumed lost in loves blind attitude at times
with withal and without
Would struggle new bravery and courage
Taming new blessed strength
To your wisest direction

The Mirror Moves
To the tapping of a drum

Waking—an aging slumber
        Already dead through decay
Into a burnt out holocaust
        Bone biting skin

The new burn out
        Programmed

Staring blindly, numbly

        Days as years

        The mirror move

        To the tapping of a drum

The Orb

Dysfunctional, Action Recall—
Synaptic Misinterpretation
            Of Intrinsic Cause and Cause of Self
Situations social or Anti-Social

            Original Creation's Teem with Fear the
                        Original Creator
            —This Information's flawed—And Built
                        In self spiting Nonsense
                        Terms
Merely in Concept though its communication
                        In Doubt

A Free Fleeting Three—dimensional thought
            And Word Speaking Tomb of
                        Terms, Confused and Abused
                        In Echoes Misused

Now a shifting uprooted Process Tree
            Cognitive Design—Full of Thoughts
                        Defining Chaos
                        Fuelled by its
            Self perpetuating misery and
                        Self loathing
                                    Inference

Succinct, Distinct,
Reaction Protocol
Between thought Modules
            Mind and Conscious
                        And my function to Survive

The filter's in Decay, stasis—Missing
                        Or Gone

The Poet of no fixed agenda

Just full of imaginary obligations
        These days
Filled with
        Endless seemingly endless time

A Reel or a lighthouse

I mean this whole passage of time
        Has only one thing in common

Take time itself—pull it apart and
        Put it back together
Expand it to
        Infinity's length
Collapse it into a
negative inversion
of itself
        Play a celestial magic trick
With it
        Argue its complete existence
            Non-existence
Re-argue its appearance and
        Disappearance

Trap it in a mind made like
        The universe
            For a year

Find out—what you knew to begin
        With
                Countless times
And what have you got?
    A waste of time

Might as well
        Wear it as a hat

The Queen Barry trust

Isolated Trapped in a psyche ward nicknamed
The queen Barry trust—by a friend
One week and boredom found the toys found claustrophobia
and destroyed parasomnia
That had planned to save the days from themselves
My mind now in clicking gears and spiting
Senses chime into pains and ailments

Queen Barry calls it home
I fight arguments from my bones
In screams crying
Run escape, lose it
But forced instead into
Mr(s) Queen barry's trust
And the wisdom of a friend

The Scrubbing

Mystic rising heated steam—
And dense smoky dream
Living in a cloud—
   A broken Prophecy
Promising scream—
   Through empty infinity

Carves, scars and highway veins—
   Naked Indian running Horse
   And leather Reigns
In a shadow's shroud—
   Infinity on trial
Permanent stains—
   Septic wounds vile

Bleach, soap, Razor brush—
   Scrubbing in naked rush
Sharpened sounds—
   The bloodied shower stream
In razor hush—
   Lost in silent scream

Torn, deep, locked hearse—
   Maddened eyes bore and rehearse
Numbed noun—
   Trappings tip a projection
Frontrunner curse—
   Liberty in reflection

Scrap, Scrap
   Some skin
      Sold for scrap
   Like Paper

The self interested signpost

In every pathway or noticing sidestep
        Of a promise or entertainment
        A heaven or Hell
        Riches or Rags
        Bells, tones, nighttime drags
            Overture melancholies
          That fills my world

Teachers in talking moods
        Or wandering caught still
My overflowing ashtrays or empty
        Bottles of blues and ill's
        Or Greens, for myself;
For those who scream only of
        Mentalistic
            Gymnastics
Against my realm of
           Semantics

A directive should be measured
        Against
        Any
           Of these
        Self interested signposts

Pushing—Pulling
        Twisting directions

(Technically better)

The mechanical animal
And his tin—foot man
Tick tock crack and scratch

The technical humanoid
And hid clockwork dream
Tip tap razor shoes

The universal mindlessness
And his dance macabre
Four four energy waves

The interpreted mis-interpreter
And his music melancholy
Deaths gentle waltzes

The invisible innocence
And his grave in E flat
Guilty beneath the bare bulb

The Very Image

Maddened by the image

       The Image is but mad
              Or Maddened
      Or Maddening
           At Least

The last resort of the contortionist
       Was to Disappear

Squirming Wheat Germ Brain
       Yeast, Ferment
      And A Garment
           For
           A Flag, Tag
           And Slag

A Waterfall Now

—You'd only notice
       If it stopped

Three Masks

Against five decorative
          Ice cubes
                    Made of silver
          In an ornamental
                    Unused Ashtray
Upon its inspection
Only

A Gentle Wind
Belligerent
                    In reminders
          Knocks occasionally
                    Against my door
But Again
Upon its inspection
                    Only

A meditation I felt a presence
          A force—an old soldiering
                    Soul return
          Wherein I laid
                    To Rest
But Again
Upon its inspection
                    Only

          Nothing At All

Tissue's and webs

Wandering Paranoia's

The mind goes mad for associations
       I have a mind
              By association

To be associated with it though
       I admit
Puts me out my mind

I'd speak my mind
       If it was mine
              But never mind

I wonder if it has any associates
       Who would?
              Associate themselves?
       With an associative mind

I caught
       Associating with me

Through loose connections
       Made in bad Habits
In a web, strung up with
       Loose connections
Associations
       In this tissue

Verb confusion

I drowned too much in silence
Suppressed long since lost
Some facts of fiction
Not fictional facts
Have slipped or snapped by
Unnoticed

The causeways filled with slogans
Brimming black with bile
A pathway crossed with bandstands
Selling stacks in vinyl

I drowned too much in silence
Fantasy—seeming itself all there was
Songs dictums dictate
Standard states
Some rivers now run dry
Unnoticed

The landfill's Smokey dank landscape
Humming blues in style
A Parapets hell bound fire escape
Smoking—A baited Breath

To commence
The ageless trial

A POETS PSYCHOSIS TAKE TWO

One twisted coin

One twisted,
>Ensnared
>>Glared and dared

Devastatingly
>In wicked glints

Its whistling choir
>Christens the air
>As it flies though
>>The shadows

Landing
>Empty in the darkness

Just faces on landing

The choice
>Still in darkness

The light nearing in
>Frenzied paces

>The end of this
>Dream

Setting a new alarm

Three days before it began—An alarm
Threw itself out the window for good
And my awoken self—Alone
Resumed its solitarily singing
No mechanisms in mind
No dreamers or souls
No minds mingle now
Let alone mangle

The time erupted into flames
I stopped forever—Never returned
To tell anyone for why
Left my work unsigned
The process still a mystery
And the reasons
Ambiguous
And Alone

The Duress
Broken by boundaries
          Borderline
          Boredomes

The Basement

The barricades of my psychosis had built over the years
The Madness and the plague
The over wash of intellectual insanities
      Materialized In a cavern of the soul
          And Mindful Mechanism
Rooted in my mind
      Organized another room
         And another writing
Desk

There—I could contemplate forever's
As they flickered past like leaves
More pages hurry—to testify a breeze
In love, harsh tones and bliss endeavors
To pace within the gentle of Ever's
Forever—Regard the tiny stories
And lose beginnings, the plots and glories
Entwine, subside then rise in together's
The scent of immortality lost in dreams
The death whispers against the skin
Old age before birth—'gainst the definition
                  I'm twinned

Swimming flash of Light
      Take the instances again
Where does time relax?

Where does time relax?
      Against its eternal self
Just clapping its hands

A Window Contrasted to a Black hole

They must both go somewhere
                                        Right
Build a box for every friend
                Loved one
                                And believer
Visiting rooms
                Observation decks
                Bedrooms and Mirrored
                                Caverns
Music rehearsal studios
                Stages
                                Theatrical sets
                                For the motionographers
Arcady
                Artist's playgrounds
Drawing boards—Unmolded clays
                                Stones, chisels
And Easels
Poet's corners
                Philosophy Libraries
                                Medicinal Centres
A Source, chamber
                Avenue and Alleyway

Infinite instancy
                Difficult one to catch

Disintegrations

I sat in a cold dreary winter upon a frozen
Bench—Aimlessly staring out across an
Ocean—To a moon with stargaze
Disintegrations—Distortions
   My eyes shatter—As the once
     Permanent stare of reality

Breaks like static
   Shuts down and dreams

   Forever now
     In only colors

Just only and only
   Do I love and loathe
   When an emotion
     Creeps
   Against my soul
Another scar wound hole

Ironically

Irony works in three's
  Lessons have themselves
And only
  Themselves

I am a speculative mechanism
Speculating upon another spindle

I learnt of,
  So long ago,
    Before the flood
Of spindles
  Three more dreams
    Again to weave
The belief of a magic
  In an impression of
    Dawn
Metaphoric,
  Allegoric,
    Realistically
Merely an Irony
  Working in three's

THE PAGES OF A
CLOWN

The Technicalities

The technical technicalities—too technical technically speaking,
Though technically I'm not technically minded,
I'm not a technician.

I've been known to be clinically technical—though not under
Clinical conditions technically, but that was dismissed
As a minor technicality.

Love, technically is not a technical thing—though my love
Is technically wrong or worse than others,
Technically that's absurd.

I sold some technical hope—because it ticked and tocked too much,
But it wasn't a clock technically, Anyway
I bought some Technical poison.

Technically I'd been poisoned—but I felt great, the doctor says
I'm dead already technically, Alas
Technically I was already dead.

Technically I've died—but I'm still around being a technical
technician
though technically, I'm not all
That technical about it.

Technically this is a poem—though technically I couldn't care
if its
Technical or not, technically its not a machine
Though it wurrs' and Burr's, technically.

Technically I should write a better one—about technicalities
Though technically thinking—this ones quite technical
Technically—Though? I'm not a technician.

A valentine's card

You're the girl that's easy!

Easy as the breeze
When you come to tease me
Please me and free me

My only warmth is found
        Through your eyes

Easy as the greening sea
The new born trees

You are nature's most
Perfect form

And with grace——I pray to all
        Gods
For each new day
        To fill me with
        Every and each new way
To strengthen our embrace

While bodies collide
        And eyes unite

I wear, swear and despise
        Each possibility

Of forsaking you

Between Pen and Paper

"This page of unfettered
Nonsense
Is amazing
Who wrote it?"

A Pen—with a taste for lies
No eyes or ties
Just a Magical Nib

"No who wrote it?
Who used the Pen?"

A Clown

A lucky one at that
If you ask me

How much can I get?
For this piece
Of impressive paper

I need more paper

"Can I buy the Pen?"

No.

Concussed Poetry

You want some more eh
        Tough guy
Now that your back
        From the dead
With that stupid Smirk

Why did you come back and how long are you going to stick
around for?

"How welcome is my visit?"

Give me another poem
        Or you're getting it in the face
And the neck
                And the cajoles
        You Fiend

"From Nobility to Servility
                Eh?"

That barely even rhymed
        And if it did
It was probably coincidence
        I'll blame the concussion
For your obvious delirium
        And subversion

I suppose there's more

"No"

Inanimate lover

I'd like to buy another rubber lover

      One who loves me this time

The last one left me
At the alter
     Crying

"How much are you willing to pay?"

      How much does true love cost these days?

"Eleven pound eighty"
     I haven't got that much
"How much do you have?"
     Just enough to be lonely
        If not less

"Well, that'll be two pound seventy"

      Would you accept—fifty seven pence, this
        Bad poem
     And I'll pay the rest
        In the next fiscal year

The Angst

Don't you understand!
     Its angst

You wouldn't understand
     Its angst

Yeah—I know this poem's crap—So what?
     Its angst

You just don't understand it like I do
     Its angst

I'm sorry if you don't understand it—if that helps
     Its just angst

I haven't got time to explain
         It's complicated
     It's Angst

How old am I—How old are you
     Its angst

The Play

With the shadow's of a doubt
I wandered out

Looking, Gazing, no care to shout
Rejected in a shadow of a doubt

I'd been drinking the day throughout
Drowning the shadow's out

Doubting the doubtless now
No shadow of a doubt

The Poem Twitches

Yea—And it gropes
        Disgusting
                Lecherous
        Thing

Talk dirty to me
Poem
After all
        I am a Whore

Trying to keep Poetic

        With this

                Penned

                Prostitute

"I Love you too Jon"

The Shotgun Wedding

A Poet at the alter, Cuffs, Bows and Laces
Stained, Drained—Inane
In a silent patience

For a bride whom he could share her pride

His being stolen—years before

A bride with loving eyes, Veiled, Immaculate in costumed graces
Embraced, brightly faced—In chase
In triggered transience

For a groom under heated stars—Souls collide

His being stolen—Years before

THE JOURNEY

Wedding Flowers

All the many weddings—Flowers, Bouquets
Banquets along the watchtower

Along the last pews in the darkness—dressed in Black
Finally for reasons—along the watchtower

As I gathered a few roses from the churchyard
Garden before processions along the watchtower

The choirs in chants of joy mock the empty
Shadowed veil mask of mine
   Here alone destroyed by the
     View of love escaping
       All along the watchtower
The thief stolen away
   With the jokers heart

A Midnight Rooster

A liars Cry
Watching it croon against the silver
Called the midnight rooster
There are no moments in Oblivion
Another side
Just a stillness with the wait and your
Seven year smile

The frozen nights
Enchanted only with out laughter
Let's praise the midnight rooster
We were young just young enough
To wait a little while
Seven years before I'd realize
Another side

The ghost and guide
Seven years denied
That life saving smile

A Plague of Locusts

The storm in breakers and chained
Lightening
        Gail's, Thunders and Tundra's,
        Cyclones
        As hard rains shatter
        Dead leaves and the debris
        Shattered onto the frozen
        Ground—the forest floor splintered

Leaving greens, blues and rose leaves
        Patterned in mosaic
        As the sunlit dawn
        Drew a light across the shadows

The shadows like locusts strived to swarm
And flutter into rest or sleep amongst
The roots of mottled trees and
The growths, mounds of fresh earth
Until the frenzied Feeding
        The next storm

The sun with crimson for the clovers
Tightening
        Strengths of the delicate
        Greenery in new genesis
        Splinter into the brazen
        Profound colors that flutter

Bursting Teal, violets and amber petals
        Growth in the meadows
        As new love fawns
        Over mother natures
            Gifts

A poets Nonsense

Jizz Jazz Jigsaw, more or less the floor
When the dizzying heights crash the ceiling fan
Or the gut wrenching lows steam in dust pans
The puzzles I make and throw pieces aside for more

Poetical nonsense comprised of less than fact
But pieced like broken gibberish or even glass
The words like toying dolls of glitter or brass
To find a poem that doesn't speak but learns to act

So if Jon is right and Jonny the remnant of my past
And time is still slow motionless and intangible
In only concept do all souls breathe in heaven's vestibule
Then shall I compact creation too swift and fast

Jonny a fool just a troubled Teen
Had Jon grew from a need to be a fresher scene
Cold showers in the morning an artifact of green
Growing older and colder in that rushing stream

Jail less now just poverty stricken for some corner cash
Exchange for some alcoholic envy and depression
Just a motor neuronal clone numb and cessation
To push past these empty months that play out brash

A Resignation Request

In the ninth Circle
        Torn by the Birds—Flesh
                In cinders
                And scars
        Before the Beast

I handed in a resignation request

        Also written in Blood

Stating how I felt there were
                More
                Opportunities
        In Marketing
        Or human resources

        I might demote
        I'll need the time
                To look after my daughter

An Exorcism

The swirling inferno—blast of energy's are
Torn from my corpse evangelist—the specter
In wild flight, escapes and is ensnared
Into the gulf of flames and into dust
      Haunts the forest in
       Its last ear piercing
          Scream

The strange friend into his departure
Torn from my corpse evangelist—the specter
And his death escapes as the fire flared
Onto the hands of flames almost just
      Judgments howl in
      The smokes steady
          Stream

An infinite Finality

In an infinite finality new beginnings emerge
To climb slowly again
        To Infinity

Love as a power into the truest understanding
Of knowledge
        —An attempt to Examine
                The Theodicy

Is one I have found for belief again
In love on earth as even
Elsewhere

Peace, Love
        And Harmony
To all life and
        God's Creatures

Before years turned to days (Minutes in an ocean)

In one blissful dreaming turning style I began to sink and sink
deeper and deeper into the dark endlessly and effortlessly
and ceasing forever I sank

I recall passing through nothingness in love with the sensations
adoring the reverberating tingling and numbing forever I sank

Lulled deeper I felt through air and water as time made
itself like an intangible echo; some kind of sound or chemical
forever still I sank

This dream in its eternal shape eventually crashing gently onto
a floor just to stop and halt the dark engulfing the scene warm
or even the tank

Here I settled my mind ata final rest of tranquility no busyness
or juggles in the oceans floor—
Before years turned to days
Minutes in an ocean
In the dream tank
Deeper I sank

Burning Leaves

The winter turning and churning in its
Cold and hail fresh chilled breeze
Swept away against the hot rush of
Smoke rolling from the burning leaves

Burning the deadened debris its
Spark and ignite the kindling sleaze
The fire soon to roar and crackle
As logs under the licking flames are seized

The clearing smashed on snow and ice
The blazing heat dampening the freeze
This tired final resting place of a
Traveling soul to where his journey's pieced
Cigarettes

Love lies and too many cigarettes
The death of liars too many stories left
I've got a girl to hold now forever
She's there to keep me safe
From my own harmful self

She's a Poet—like many lovers are
I'm a lover—like many losers are
She can't lose—Too much of a fighter
I've lost it all—Cant fly much higher
      Than the sinking depths
      Of nothingness
      No other High

Cosmic Guru's

I once self stylized and made a custom
        Set of limited edition
        Jon Sutcliffe
                Divination, Tarot and
                Playing cards
For a game of solitaire
        And a short film called
                Distraction
Three months later I'd uncovered
        Secrets of the Universe
But I still wasn't distracted
Enough
I called the Hanged Man
                A Poet
And the magician
                The Joker

        Drew up three Jacks
And called the poet an Ace

Then bought Five Jokers to pair
With each card
Individually
As five players

Put the Five original Cards
        In a river

And played a stupider game
        Of solitaire
Similar to Poker

Drunk, for my lonely
        Twenty third Birthday

Divine Intervention

In the constancy—My desperation
          Has grown to be
      My mind adamant to convince
        Myself

I have been to my birth
      And have been to my death
But have I been the darkness
      That surrounds, Engulfs
          And at desperate times
      Will inevitably
        Swallow me

I turn to a God
      And imagine her
        All over again
      And I am given another song

Dragons Eyes

I'll remember pretty faces forever in jealousy
Some names just hurt to recall
Most angels fly by—fly by night
No missing pieces—No dragon's eyes

She wanders in and out of dreams for energy
Some chases just break into a crawl
Loving devils drop out—and deepen the plight
To Jag up edges—The Dragons eyes

Catch the one who wants to get caught naughtily
Some nymphs just want to enthrall
Never a Dragon flies right—or land in spite
They chase water with their tails and eyes

Drowning, Le deluge

Staggering now In a dream's disguise

      Dog faced dragons
            Crackons
      And other mythologies

Humor's mistake to
      Make farce of escape

Was a last laugh riot
      Fought in tears

Now—When— One man's pain
         One clown's gesture
         One Poet's pride
         One fool's façade
         One lover's labor lost
         One monk's vow stolen
         One profit's Poverty

All becoming one again
A past, Now to endure
Within tamed memory
      Alone

With each Poison, Venom, Vile and bile
      Of A tortured soul
Exited through a dusty lavatory bowl

Shall he now leave
      And never return

Hiding in Skins

Deep into the core of bone a slither of a soul
Hangs by a silver thread bare to its former
Self now made a shell and parasite
Host to wandering consciousness
And the touches of angels
And devils
Each other—Taking turns
Spite the lord's work

Deep in a torn and shredded heart a glimpse of love
Floats like coy carp like transience its former
Stranger love made timid or of deep
Waiting for bait and feasting
Of lovers touches pure
And impure
Each other—taking turns
All in loves work

Deep in a mangles manacled mind a pearl of
Contention seeks retention of its former
Clarity and its intellectual charities
Wisdom, learnedness and tricks
Of ageing words serious
And Jest
Each other—Taking turns
Despite the minds work

Till these re-emerge
I'm just hiding in skins

IOU's

The Iou's I sold In hope not to lose
The very last
Of what I had left
After I had lost it all

The Ious I owed Signed with hope to prove
The least of
Good intentions
But that was
After all

The Iou's I spun With lust luck and love
The lovers
Repaid in full
Hey Ho
And after all

The Ious I used Upon us and you
Lasts another
Million years
Soon very soon
I'll collect them all

The Ious I burnt With foreign cigars
Ashes for
Ashtrays
Into breezes
After all

The lous I built Into paper planes
Re-paying back
Some spirits
Sea's and gulls
And salt

The lous I made Valued by the word
Spoke, forsaken
Mistook and took
For those still
After all

And after all

La Lune

To praise a goddess—a spirit or muse
As she meditates my night time tranquility
With the harmonies of gentle rhymes
—

We speak of moments—the days and news
As she proposes all loves and proper prosperity
To plan a refuge for my only darkest times
—

She sings and croons—songs of love and use
Sending scribbled scraps of hope against futility
And joins the melodies with a love entwined
—

Now in her waxing—the growth and boost
To her full shining glory in her powers utility
So I find a noble strength as we align

She catches my writing—finds it very curious
And sometimes finding it funny often sad
Never judging my nighttime companion
—

She sings in soft harmonies—of the music as;
I often attempt as well, together we sing
Of love the future past and loves reunion
—

Over years it's a midnights silvery ties that
Bind us now in the gentlest of nights
For the waxing and waning and turning the moon on
—

I miss her in June—La Lune when we are
Apart the most, to praise a goddess a spirit
Or muse never in ritual but magic conversation

Like trying to get water on a page

Holiday making rainmaker
        Haymaker
        Flight plan faker
            Forsaken Taker
Of a bad noise and senseless sound

Beyond years burnt
        Again the realm turned

As a frozen baron dream
        Against dust bowl storms
        And a hurricane warning

Tore a travelers check
        From a cloak
            Turned into dust
Love and Life in a cigarette

So?—Another Poem Eh?

Imposing upon me the position
An Improper Imposter
Of a little chord
Sang in Ink
Finitely—for a definite
Indelible
Perhaps this time intelligible

Notion of proper Disposal

Or is a must
This haunting riddle
Stay Just
The Carnival of dust

Spins
the spindle
Jingles
Wrangled

The Laughter
The Haunting
Laughter

Love is upside down this time

Love is upside down this time
       It is not the right way up this time

Her incessant needs for love and compassion
       A devils touch at night
            And an angelic tongue to match

       Were amongst the many possessions
          I had lost—inside of myself
              Alone

A love for her is all I had to
Set her free
       Into Meadows and
             The lives
         Of the Hapless animals
          Lovers become
   I—Alone—For love

Love is upside down now
       It is not the right way up
When the moment arrived,
         And the news
       Of her—dying love
            For me
Came out on a note,
       A lover's eulogy
An epitaph

For love this time, that time
Was upside down
   It is not the right way up
   Though I loved her so
   And let her go
     And forever

Nihilist Screams

I found a clearing
Some trees
And the earth was warm
The nestling sensation
Clinging to worms

I found a nearing
Disease
And the hearth was torn
The rumble reverberation
As thinking squirms

I found a flicker
Flying
And the sky was free
The trembling sound
And thunder

I found doubles
Lacking
The night was bleak
The dreaming

Norse Fables

Valhalla,
>   Heaven
>   The Islands of the Blessed
This collection
>   Of gilded stars to its breast
The Darkness
>   Pounds and opens the Vaults
The Raptures
>   Hoard these floating souls
>> Incarta, incorporeus

My time, life aside
>   Against measured silence
Is a shape
>   With no edges
>> A sycamore seed
>   Creating hurricanes
>> With the air

Obituaries

Flower arrangements and decorative floral roasters
Along the rear of a hearse and in the arms of
The procession along banks by the river

The river slipping through banks as a stream but
Deeper—the rushing water pacing with the
Procession faster but timed—respect—death from the river

At the final bend as the river turns into the wider
Estuary the hearse and March move with the lane
The procession a half mile till resting with the river

If I prepared eighteen Fake deaths in a journey across all
Countries and planted a paper trail of obituaries
And graves with pseudonyms—I could never disappear
        As easy as the water

            That comes as rain
                    To become the river
                    And get lost in the ocean

            An Ocean of many dead and ancient
            Creatures—of no obituaries
            Just fed from estuaries

"Pedestal"

She took him from his pedestal then strangled him to death.
The crowd watched in unison synchronizing breath.
The Birds began to scatter North east south and west.

It was not he who sought to be what he would soon become
It was fate and stars that formed the bars a prison now
undone.

She took him from his pedestal then strangled him to death.
Lost reasons later fled before he came to rest.
The wind chose not to howl and scream of its bereft.

It was not he who sought to be the evil of all men
It was that and this that built up slow and rose into his skin.

She took him from his pedestal then strangled him to death.
Dawn was nearing and for her, there was nothing left.
But to take this poor and shambled man whose tragedy was
his Jest.

And take him from his pedestal and strangle him to death.

Poem's from a drawing

In the silver strewn
        And sorrow stem
                Shadowed
In the heart of this forest
        And Grave

The rope—And noose
Prepared for a poised
        Precise Purpose
An accused, Misused—
       Now Refused

Position of Proposal
To this chosen ceremony

While Thunders, No Lightning
The storm like a soldier
The breeze a bombardier
Trustling leaves—The hymns

In straws of silk Rags
        And paper hearts
              Hollowed
In the heart of this forest

Where promises and sentences
        Have confused themselves
           Into One

Poetic Licenses

Plagorisms
      Subliminations
          And Gibberishisms
Some Neologisms
     Skisms in
Chasms

Dropping into a Box
     The Temple
         Pentathon

For a conversation
Peaceful Protagonisms
In Arguments
Debates

With my own
Infinite
        Selves
And A Trap door
Through Nowhere
To the Somewhere

I'll never reach myself

The Happier Place

Ravens

I was losing, out of my mind
When the angels flew by
Reaching out for me at that time
Though ravens can't die

I was lost and I was broken
Somewhere in my mind
So the angels will fly
Until the raven will die
In the somewhere of my mind

Id lost it all, nothing new to find
The raven never said goodbye
Never came back to tell me why
The reason ravens can't die

In the loss, broken
My confused mind
So the raven can't die
She flew on by
Making angels cry

Im somewhere lost in time
Somewhere in my mind

Recoveries, Rivalries and Revelries

Foreign Tears arrove along with the tunes
Of birds singing—An hour before
Midnight on a Christmas Eve

And stained the page of the ragged scrap
Poetries (bleeding)—This pain soft
And in no warning to perceive

The stony face and deadened stare seemed
Cruel against the tears—I felt absurd
For the small emotion made for me

Quietly as if a protective force had found me
A tear was shed in grief—Loss, woe
And pity for my soul

Foreign tears burned alone with purity
Of angel's blessings—but again I brushed
The magic away—and spat Acid
                    And spite
                    Hateful poison
]   Upon my most recent poem's

                    Impotency

Roses

Red Red Roses
Colored by the Sun
Like Wine
I'm Drunk

Dead Dead Dreams
Gone in the Hum
Like Time
I'm Drunk

The Breeze and Beauty
And I am Caught
Wind Sweep me free

Whirlpool Girl
Summer Dress on
You Shine
I'm Drunk

She just She

She prays for pennies not love
And the angels scream at my only
Solitude—as she lets it grow

She caught me in a prison
The torturers driving pits to hells high
Waters—as she lets it flow

She stole my body destroyed it
Left me in the cruel world she learned
To idolize—as demons begin to moan

A new world now torn to death
From her throne As I in evils way
Left alone—as beaten shadows are blown

My broken self and soldier's stone
The soul a mercenary to a world beyond the
Grass grown—stolen souls through horizons flown

Treading the two year sentence of hell on earth
Gently floating over sins and treachery like an
Angel—Against a hanging alone

Scorn

It's the only truth—was or
Had I not been met with
Her scorn—Attempting my suicide
For her—alone to benefit
—I admit I would have
loved once

Languish

The pacts that were made
In my occultist ways
No reward
        And no power
No Harm and no
Influence—Just
Company—and a
        Visit on Earth

Inventions

Absolution itself provides
No solution—a long decay
Into death—upon arriving
Only unto inspection
No other absolution
Is as cruel
As perceivable
        Perfection

Metaphors

All that I see
Amongst these leaves
Flickering
The Autumn Breeze
These Moments
Familiar,
Just mine and ours
In recurring
      Metaphors

Scorn

The finishing lines—
Now in current definitions
Alone, infinite
        Or meaningless

Them

Did I recall once I tried
To find me—but never
Could, did I just
Plan self revenge
Against a
        Self slaughterer

Selves

Matchsticks
on shelves

Snapping Branches

Into this furnace——I condemn
    This condensation
The lapse of Incredibility
    And its
    Opportunistic abilities
Without the look of locking bolts
    Upon the mouth
    Of a smoker

The branches
    Dead and chilled
In the winter
    Would complain

With the heat nestling in the heart
Of the soil, the blaze in its
Repetitious swirl, the hypnotized
Tracks left in the half settled
Snow, The Oak and willow
The whistling brook and the
Final harmony was
A final reward

For a steward

A Poet of no
Fixed Agenda

Sothic, Solaris, Eclipse

Sirius—Deep into the brine, A Castor Blue
        Its Tides,
                Bright
                            Pale Cast
Flooding the universe
        As an Arena
Solaris and chariot
                Arrives
        In a double twinned Eclipse

Swimming in the shallows

Along the Journey on the warmest break in the brisk Autumn I strove into the shore head the quarter mile to the lowest tide of the month and placing my clothes neatly on the wooden head of a bay for boats and dock—Into the darkening sea and horizon I dove and prepared for a long swim in the shallows. For durations and lengths till the muscles burning overwhelmed the bitter cold and the blood like ice began to boil and bleed through the veins and heart. The ocean was baron and bleak deceptively lifeless swimming like clockwork the strokes like brushstrokes making patterns in the otherwise still waters.

The swim in the shallows a nothingness but an elucidated metaphor against a bobbing mane of blackening hair—perfectly setting itself against the dusk settling off into the sea's horizon with the retiring sunset—As the warm waters begin to chill the swimmer rides the current back to the dock and bay rises and dresses.

Slowly again dry now and preparing further along the journey takes a cigarette from a satchel and lights it in the beginning of the nights thick blanketing darkness—smoking now and drinking heavy from a flask of dry Gin, traveling the night again, swimming in its shallows.

Tandem Bicycles

Tandem Bicycles climbing backwards upstairs
They say true loneliness comes in pairs
While love itself
Was in love with the world and alone

The choice for a soldier is how much time to kill
The choice for a drunk to let his thirst stand still
Only mine is stained—Against a moonlit tide
For a failure of mine
That they can only breathe and alone

And while my breath with my absent sin
Their going to catch me let my noose begin
To wrangle and knot
My feet dancing with the wind and alone

Cycling forever around a broken moon
      The high tide noon
      The lapse of something new
          And alone

Tattoo's for Talons

The flight of a bird—of either pray, power or prayer
Scorched the skies with grace, destiny
    And into the depths of a
    Downward turn—handling
    The skyway with ease;
Of a shark on hunt
    Or lemur on leap
    Or a pack of piranha's in frenzy's
        For a floundering
            Buffalo

The heights so absurd—the plunge, poise and stare
Torched the frightening pace, chastity
    And onto the strengths of a
    Vertical burn—tumbling
    In spirals with the ease;
Of a deer bucking the brunt
    Or the herding of sheep
    Or the climbing of spiders in trees
        For the Spinning

The Nests,
    Webs,
        Glens
        All habitats
    For and of natures beauty

    All the Tattoo's for Talons

The Arrows

In the dawn,
As the fire finally fell
The smoke as dust
Rising from the
Smoldering Ashes
      The Charred wood and its
            Embers
      Charging into the soil

Great Pan in thickets
Arranging trickery
With Achilles and his Archers

Twenty three Arrows
From the fire—to the tips of Roots

Shot from gnarled and knotted Bark

In penetration to swell
      My Heart
And cast it in stone
Green—I fell back
      And laid unconscious
in the leaves

The Collections

52 Cards, 36 Scars, 22 Songs from Broken Guitars
13 Ghosts, 78 Hosts, 98 Leeches Bridges and Moats
3 Masks, Limitless Tasks, 1 Green Mottled Hip Flask
5 in a River—2 in play—Joker and Thief

99 Dreams, each with screams, 69 stitches for torn out seams
Dead Matchsticks, clicks and tricks, Poems born from Guitar Picks
Crackled Tapes, Distant Escapes, Some Sand, Pebbles and
Handpicked Grapes
5 in a river—2 in play—Jokes and Hearts

Hoards of Demons, Shadows Lunge, A two storey Hole and
Car Park
Formless Image, Changing shape, these too closely infinitely
break
3 False Teeth, burning leaves, and all the fire you couldn't
keep
5 in a river—2 in play—Ace over Jacks

No Idea's, Scattered Fears, dousing enflamed hearts endless
tears
Bottled bread, covers and beds, Pills and Gange filled Sheds
15 lists of gist's and mists, torturous tongue twists
5 in a river—2 in play—Jacks over Jacks over Jacks

The Burning School

After the delay I'd caused believing
I was delayed
Then delaying to check again

To measure how long I'd been
Delayed by
Then I checked time twice
     The delay thrice
And considered the difference
Between the two
For too long a time

And left the burning school
     A single partisan
          To the broken Religion
     Accidentally created

     The Lock Shattered
     The Key town in two

I returned to the institute I'd
Dropped out of—so unrighteously

Because of my mental Health

The School I'd burnt
     The Bridges to
But not the moats

The Music of spring and Magpies

The silver of the moon—Swept away with Tides
To clean the canvas Dry
And Room now enough to swing
In the music of spring

The Blaze of Crimson Stars—Extinguished
Lost, In the Sun's old glory
Children glinting in the sharp eyes
The Magic of Magpies

The Pedestal before Dawn

I, realizing In an Ocean's floor
Basins, Boil and blood—the soar
Of Gall's gusts and death
The Breath now Broken

Better Soulless Now
        Dreamless, Mindless
And No hope left now

A Newer stronger loneliness
And silence
        Tight and Taut like
        An unbroken in
                Drum

        Still Ready

The rebels leaflet

Isn't it harsh?
     To watch a technical
          Nothingness
Built only for its destruction
When all of reality's
     Outside in Rebellions
     Self served death plane realm

I'll return alone stabbed
     By an Idea
     Or a dream
          Again

Bleeding,
     Broken,
          Through no Blindness
     Sell the self serving cycles
     For saviors
          And
          Saving graces

The love I've offered
     Is only a life taker
I promise to give these lives back
     Pristine
          And perfect

The Self Collection

The Shards and Fractured
Pieces of my
Plane glass
Shattered Mind

Swept in a hail and
        Thunders

Hurricane Souls
        Binded Tight
        And Taught

To Perfection

Like a full august
Moon

She found me—where I
Landed
        I Felt empty
        Immediately Warmed

        In her Embrace

Then Drained
        I could rejoice
            Again
        And Felt
        My eyes flood
with life

"The Sorrow Stem—
(in shame I met defeat)"

The drowning inaudible invincible defeat,
And a lack of time for Rhymes.

Saw just above the waves—
As bubbles burst, and splashes of splashes are more silent.
A fear that washes, rides a wave, and ebbs as echoes—
Crashing waves—
Yet now more silent still.

Dark caverns lay deep within the sounds,
The jutted mangling of the mind.

As glassy eyes could gander—
From further than I could reach—

I felt my defeat.

The growing insoluble magnificent defeat,
And a lack of rhymes for crimes.

Saw just above the waves—
As lightning crack, and thunders of thunders are more silent.
A dream that deepens, loves to die, and cries as human—
Weeping waves—
Yet now more silent still.

Bleak Sky—way's broke free within the sounds,
The jutted mangling of the mind.

As broken eyes did gander—
From further than I could reach—

I knew my defeat.

The screaming inculpable innocent defeat,
And a lack of crimes for minds.

Saw just above the waves—
As shadows creep, and whispers of whispers are more silent.
A Birth that scorns, brought to mourn, and dies as chosen—
Teasing waves—
Yet now more silent still.

Calm night-time struck Chords within the sounds,
The jutted mangling of the mind.

As Galled eyes should gander—
From further than i could reach—

Iknew my defeat.

The passing indelible scarring defeat,
And a lack of mind for time.

Saw just above the waves—
As troubles dawn, and faces of faces are more silent.
A shame that stems, grows to feed, and pricks as thistles—
Tidal waves—
Yet now more silent still.

Brisk morning caught sight within the sounds,
The jutted mangling of the mind.

As Sorrowed eyes will gander—
From further than I could reach—

I knew again and revealed my defeat.

The spitting silence and Hissing Hills

Along a west coast, irish sea and a traveling cloak—leather and unstudded no flag or shield—spiting the scorned winds with curses and slurs. The drunk tolls of a nowhere march in shoes burnt by fire and dusty earth and soaked in water. The haunting howls at night, the ancient stare to the low far tides; the brisk pace set with rising suns, moons the ebb of the waves—The solitude now against the screams and caws of seagull's magpie's and raven's another chiming symphony—this journey under no weight of a plan or purpose. An empty walk through the park of life in no more traces the paces filling the voids of my mind with rhythm, past causeways, fjords and estuaries the seaside towns and arcades and shops; the stranger wander off into their own lives away from my often maudlin march—into their homes, homesteads communities and businesses—with each setting sun bringing the chill with every noon the warmth forever to continue again.

Along the coast with its tamed and timed nature its shapes and sounds, the hours to days, the days to weeks and within a month at the foot of a hill—An arduous climb nothing but sweat and salt to raise a limp body and mount it on the climb—at the peak standing alone with the metaphor and a frenzied haze of euphoria, just now to roar against

The Spitting Silence and Hissing Hills

That I eventually returned

Alone

The Taste

Sweet tastes entwine themselves
        And continue to want
        Things such as lust
            And others

Are consummations built?
        Before and Against
        Nothing made—except in a
           Glory of—?

This
        I must confess

        ;—Do you think your just
        Another guy in the world?

My response as I caught
        Myself
           Was

Yes—I certainly feel
        Like one
        Right here—
           Along my thigh

The Universal

One mysterious night I strove into the depths
Of my mind to find an oasis blazing
                              In Fire

The burning oasis—trees tear smoke like
Tornado's deeper into the stratosphere, the
Lake boils, burns and scalds the sand—
Melting into dense black rock and onyx
—Never to be chiseled just rough cut sharp
And troublesome to tread upon

In the pit of the island idyllic landscape a
Thunder roared from its core and the trees
Now burnt and splintered—shattered and
All beauty corroded—A volcano's activity
Forced to the surface and the oasis began
Twisting, twisting into a supernova like
A star exploding—
The debris compacted into nothingness
—Then the Novocain Erupts

My mind now consumed the explosion the
Whole space, surrounding and filling every
Crevasse—The debris in carnage and chaos
Slowly forming into order and pattern—A
Newer universe and heaven or hell forged
From fire and death—sure that it'll soon settle
And grow one year away from the oasis
Again another form of self that'll
Never out grow its very self

The Oasis exploding to become
A mind itself or a universe

Three Priests

In a chambered temple
  Awoken in separate rooms
  Three priests of separate
      Replicate
  And of identical virtues
Met three
  Of the makers
      Of manhood

And took them along three
  Journeys
  Through lives
      Days
      And ages
      And nights
Till reawaken
  Reunited
  At its gates
  For departure

Three second impacts

I get turned on,
      And chase women
On impact,
      Impression
          And Afterthoughts

I've been forever left alone
      Unnoticed, unloved and forever
      Forsaken—as a stranger
Unimpressionable
      A Ghost or Shadow
      Easily passed over
      For any other
          Stranger

Lucky enough
      With the chance
Entwining the gentle threads
      More perfectly

The three seconds of
      An Impact

POEMS FROM A
PUPPET

Wild

Wilting wild flowers are all I know
Trying to second guess the shapes that grow
Yet its nature's chaos that's let me go—but anyway
Tell me—How it got to this—Anyway

And all the joy rings like bells
Manic laughter too, hurts like hell
Yet its only timing, that'll let me know—but anyway
Tell me—How it got to this—Anyway

Girl its damaged my mind—to think of you this way
I'm vain and senseless—and a fool to wasted hate
I hope at least your smiling when you walk away
But I bet you won't

The pain now so far removed
The jump for a high flier tombed
Its near dawn and Im letting go—But anyway
Tell me—How it got to this—Anyway

Dignity

It was in the coldest of the harsh lights of his final day
He tore apart the voodoo mask and broken throne

And gathering his soul back in magick's from the debris and
decay
Bought with himself the blessings of a palace of bone

Alone now though his heart broken and thoughts dismayed
He was redeemed and content humbly again all alone

His father had understood that time and life would always
fray
Yet to his mother was the soul to be owned

Broken and cold, bare and in need—awash with breathing
snow
In torn rags after being witness to the cruelty of life

In a garden behind his only home the dying night letting go
After his many years since the death of his only wife

In his old age, his time ravaged and burned like a heavy
candle glow
Troubled with the weight of heavy bones and strife

Sure that when he finally died would find peace but could
never know
He looked to the stars and heavens for the lord to ignite

Distances

When I stared from that desolate vice made of ice, static
Death decay and the chains on the blades mirror edges and
a shadowy decoy and my eyes died, dried as all the blinking
stopped to destroy

Was it her hurt some pain some scars she's got by her thighs its
all just pride she's just as done over by pride and the torture
when her soul cannot hide

These distances now drag on magnet poles into caverned holes till
freedom her escape onto distant lands locked islands with entrance
fees costs freedom while im trapped inside her trick devilishly
caught between the crucifixion and mocked Christendom

Then the talk the talk she got rolled over by talk least of it
mine I couldn't mind its all just pride done over again by talks
of pride she's with another now all others and with her soul

At last—Another only resort
Well I could fade into a green—it'd be obscene
Well I could swell into a void—it'd drown the noise
Well I could reappear alone—back into that nowhere
        Throne—someone cursed upon me
Well I could drown into a bottle—and love and apologize
from that hearse

Sometime later I chased her down quick as a dog and bitten
with lusts desire for revenge blood curdling thirst
Setting scores and Olympian records in rain making the lover
colliding crashes of moans and screams lusts blood curdling thirst

The locked away dreamer stirred the specters all burned in an
ageless orgasm as the sweat salted my tongue as she writhed
and threw me into existence

That past sin kept crawling under flesh the beast of a whore
chilled like a tempest winter storm the hurt
Burst with a rising heat a Novocain euphoria of pain in a
release and more ecstasy reeled and writhed with the blood
curdling thirst

The locked away dreamer screamed stirred an echo of its
primitive self into a cruel reality into the throngs of passion
and thrown back into existence

Grasshopper

Another manic grasshopper lucid dream
A gun locked nightmare in its own design
Awake and awash now premature and pristine

The masks of mud slow and lost in its decays
Intercept the pores of a face burnt
As moisturizers embalm the frays

The fire and plague that tore my broken slumber
Shattered scars of fear into the eyes and mind
Dawn now and a safety returns in her

As she turns and stirs destruction collapses
In her warm embrace then faded and turned
My useless features now in abscences

Insomnia

Honey, my minds missing from my eyes
My severed soul praying in a trance
The space age is a holocaust in disguise
I'll trade her fortune for all your romance

And I don't want to lie
But the truth scares me

So any special wishes
Before I go
Any kind regards
From the valley below

The famous blue sky tore apart
And I could fathom a Lord
Before my years turned to dust
The rope and noose toed up and bored

Come and watch me bleed
So much it scares me

So any special wishes
The darkened windows
Any fantasy from
The thorny Gallows

And as snowfell I grew cold
I made a mask out of snow
Grew new eyed from its water
And saw the birth of my old soul

Locked Jaws

Until the canvas dries the scars dissolve and shed from the
now in turning skins shed and shear—blown and burnt off and
fresh in the holocaust winds grown again like leather bound
books and alternate edition
Cursed in its creation by the destruction in process in a world
of heavens above hells below they can only creep unto the
earth and play the games out for real in a realm to tame
Divine or sublime the new skin for the earth and flesh alone
until the canvas dries the fighting of fear is its own subliminal
protagonist in us all a few denials to emotions need breeding
are all that my former self in isolation suffering false
convictions and trials a martyrdom not religious
Now dirty Jazz no smooth slow blues and locked jaws some
say half of life is what you can get away with and the other
half—the accidental impossibilities we achieve the masks
and facades—tiny vehicles the world gave us to survive may
explode someday suffering submissions to achieve the nobler
aspects of ourselves
Until the canvas dries
        And dried to decay

Puppets

Pulling Puppets on their strings
Unhinged I drowned and lost the screams
Silence drives through the giant causeway of nights
As flights of no consensus drop into stage frights

While distant screams from Cyrus
The nimbus damped dawns fresh and clean
Lay the puppet on his pedestal
One perfect pretence of his dreams

To only just obscure obscenities in scenes

Watch the tortured twisting damning specters
Tear and ravage at its screams
And a wooden Horse like pitch pipe cry
That floods arena's in streams
As silence flights fly away into madness
The damning wrangling of strings

So?—Another Poem Eh?

The Joints burn, the Jaw won't turn
The limbs jut and never cease
My body tears and writhes in pain
Every time the possessions cease
Do I collapse and cry in tears
Broken just to breathe
Broken—Just to breathe

Button eyed—stitched up to dance
     And Jump—Barking Orders
     At me and nothing else

When am I to be lowered and freed?
     Just broken—Just to breathe

Scars from demonic faceless villains
Have left me here morbid and stained
Noted
     Just as faceless
Broken—Just to breathe

Spider

The spiders climbing from the torn
Seems, the edges of eyes
The darkened forest where I rested
Amongst the autumn decayed leaves
The haunted self of the life
A mangled stranger the corpse in love
Creatures and eyes devoted in the darkness
To lust the flesh and scent
A risen in the birth of magic to float
Ceaselessly tired though bent
As a night dreams and dawn implores
Its gentle rest and cycle
The dew damped breeze and beauty
Erupts from chaos and life
In the Smokey dust banks of a retired
Fire the smoke stained clothes
Of a stranger stenches the slow
March to the edge of the woods
Chasing drunken shadows after
The dancing and ceremony as they
Continue to relish in the strangers
Madness

The institute

How did I manage Sunday—drinking my soul away?
The devil may care someday—against angels who sway
The institutes on fire—And Heavens broken Gaze

Can only call on the righteous—with a pious tongue
To save the meek and meager—from a loose head run

How did I save the last of—the blues I saved?
Digging holes too deep for—my shallow grave
And destinies in Tandem—Hell is all ablaze

Will she shatter this silent night—with an almighty scream
Or pick apart this puzzle—at its tears and its seams

When life gets too lonely—disappearing with no trace
And I left it all in ruins—trying to save some face
Now its on a funeral pyre—and my minds just a haze

If I tore down this broken wall—laid it once to waste
Instead of swallowing darkness—with its addictive taste

The Jack of Spades

The twisting jump of the jack of spades,
While the forest nurses lakes and glades,
Nirvana's peak in bleak retire,
Causing rains against loves fire,
The forlorn desire in Heartbeats dire
Death in straits and pounding for the
The ace

On a landing crash,
The destiny smashed,
The ice shattered now into a deep embrace,
The Jack turns to sport his face,
The torn mask in heartbeats dire
Death in straits and pounding for
The Queen

The lapse of a hoarded vanity,
Erupts against beauty's profanity,
Shangri La's heaven and sun spoilt hills,
By the locked Jaws of losers and pills,
The hope in sweat drips and burns
From pores and founding for
The king

The old return of the once then burnt,
The king lay in a spring time turned,
The seasons in grinding gears,
Nobility no smiling fears,
To bring the peace of rolling years,
The tired breath in heartbeats dire
Death in straits and pounding for
The Jack of spades

The twisting jump of shy charades